DINOSAURS COUNT!

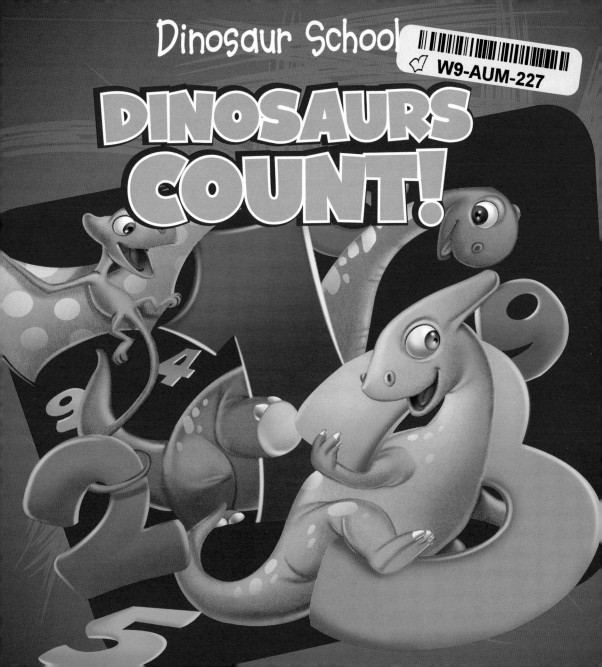

Please visit our website, www.garethstevens.com. For a free color catalog of all our high-quality books, call toll free 1-800-542-2595 or fax 1-877-542-2596.

Library of Congress Cataloging-in-Publication Data

Saviola, Ava.
Dinosaurs count! / Ava Saviola.
    p. cm. — (Dinosaur school)
ISBN 978-1-4339-7152-5 (pbk.)
ISBN 978-1-4339-7153-2 (6-pack)
ISBN 978-1-4339-7151-8 (library binding)
1. Counting—Juvenile literature. 2. Dinosaurs—Juvenile literature. I. Title.
QA141.3.S378 2013
513.2'11—dc23

2011048208

First Edition

Published in 2013 by
Gareth Stevens Publishing
111 East 14th Street, Suite 349
New York, NY 10003

Copyright © 2013 Gareth Stevens Publishing

Designer: Ben Gardner
Editor: Kerri O'Donnell

All illustrations by Planman Technologies

Printed in the United States of America

CPSIA compliance information: Batch #CS12GS: For further information contact Gareth Stevens, New York, New York at 1-800-542-2595.

DINOSAURS COUNT!

By Ava Saviola

Gareth Stevens
Publishing

one

I see one dinosaur.

two

I see two dinosaurs.

three

I see three dinosaurs.

four

I see four dinosaurs.

five

I see five dinosaurs.

six

I see six dinosaurs.

seven

I see seven dinosaurs.

eight

I see eight dinosaurs.

nine

I see nine dinosaurs.

ten

I see ten dinosaurs!

Dinosaurs Count

one

two

three

four

five

six

seven

eight

nine

ten

24